DAYBOOK

OF CRITICAL READING AND WRITING

daybook, *n.* a book in which the events of the day are recorded; *specif.* a journal or diary

THE AUTHORS
* Laura Robb
* Michael F. Opitz
* Ellin Oliver Keene

Great Source Education Group
A division of Houghton Mifflin Company
Wilmington, Massachusetts

THE AUTHORS

✳ **Laura Robb** has more than forty years of classroom experience in grades 4 through 8. Robb also coaches teachers in grades K to 12 in school districts in her home state of Virginia, New York, and Michigan and speaks at conferences throughout the country. Author of more than fifteen books for teachers, Robb's latest title is *Teaching Reading: A Complete Resource for Grades Four and Up* (Scholastic, 2006). For Great Source, Robb has developed, with other authors, *Reading Advantage, Writing Advantage,* and *Reader's Handbook* for grades 3 to 8.

✳ **Michael F. Opitz** is a professor of reading at the University of Northern Colorado, where he teaches graduate and undergraduate literacy courses. He is the author or coauthor of several books, including *Diagnosis and Improvement in Reading Instruction,* 5th ed. (Allyn & Bacon, 2007); *Books and Beyond* (Heinemann, 2006); *Listen, Hear!* (Heinemann, 2005); and *Goodbye Round Robin* (Heinemann, 1998) as well as the reading programs *Afterschool Achievers: Reading Club* (Great Source, 2004) and *Literacy By Design* (Harcourt, 2007).

✳ **Ellin Oliver Keene** has been a classroom teacher, staff developer, and adjunct professor of reading and writing. For sixteen years, she directed staff development initiatives at the Denver-based Public Education & Business Coalition. She served for four years as deputy director and director of diteracy and staff development for the Cornerstone Project at the University of Pennsylvania. Ellin is coauthor of *Mosaic of Thought: Teaching Comprehension in a Readers' Workshop* (Heinemann, 1997), the second edition of which was released in 2007. She is also the author of *To Understand* (Heinemann, 2007) and *Assessing Comprehension Thinking Strategies* (Shell Educational Books, 2006).

REVIEWERS

Cheryl Fox Dultz
Citrus Heights, CA

Cynthia Fontenot
Lafayette, LA

Pickett Pat Lema, EdD
St. Louis County, MO

Mary Osborne
Largo, FL

Pamela J. Strain
Rosemead, CA

EDITORIAL: Ruth Rothstein and Sue Paro
DESIGN AND PRODUCTION: AARTPACK, Inc.

Printed in the United States of America

International Standard Book Number 13: 978-0-669-54977-5

International Standard Book Number 10: 0-669-54977-0

1 2 3 4 5 6 7 8 9 10 - VH - 12 11 10 09 08 07

Contents

Focus / Skill	Selection / Author	

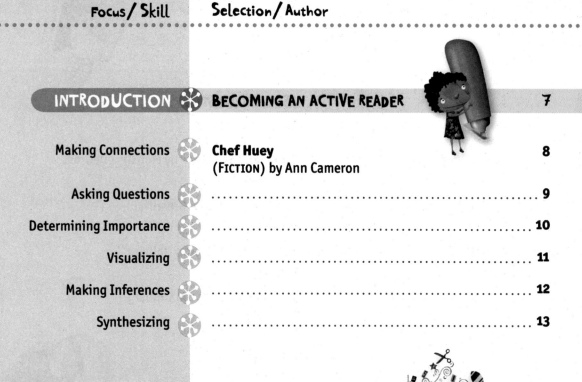

Focus/Skill	Selection/Author	

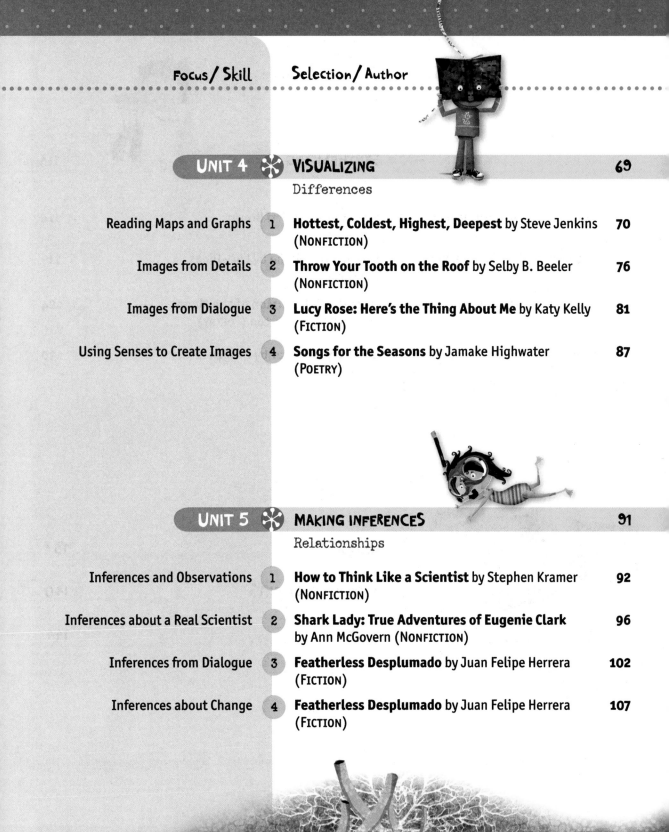

Focus / Skill	Selection / Author	

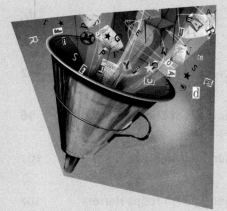

Becoming an Active Reader

Reading is a lot like playing soccer. The more you read actively, the better you'll get. As an active reader, you interact with the text by thinking, writing, and talking about it.

The strategy lessons in this *Daybook* will build your reading power. In each unit, you'll interact with the text by making connections, asking questions, determining importance, visualizing, making inferences, and synthesizing. By actively using these strategies, you'll find that you understand, remember, and enjoy more of what you read.

When you read, look for ideas and details that remind you of things you already know. This is called **making connections.** Making connections with a text will help you better understand and remember what you read. Make connections by asking questions such as these:

- What does this remind me of?

- Where have I seen or heard this before?

Practice making connections with this part of "Chef Huey." Mark the text by underlining phrases or sentences that remind you of things you already know. Write about your connections in the **Response Notes.**

Response Notes

I invented a new food once!

from Chef Huey by Ann Cameron

"Food should be different from the way it is," I said to my mom. "Then I wouldn't mind eating it."

"How should it be different?" my mom asked.

"I don't exactly know," I said.

"Maybe you will figure it out and be a chef," my mom said.

"What's a chef?" I asked.

"<u>A chef is a very good cook who sometimes invents new things to eat,</u>" my mom told me.

The next day we went to the supermarket. I saw pictures of chefs on some of the food packages. They were all smiling. I wondered if when they were little they had to eat what their parents told them to eat. Maybe that's why they became chefs—so they could invent foods that they liked to eat. Probably that's when they became happy.

Ask questions before, during, and after reading. **Asking questions** keeps you interested in the reading because you search for the answers. Through questioning, your thinking becomes clearer.

As you read, ask questions such as these:

- What will happen next?

- Why did that character do that?

- Why did the author include (or not include) those details?

As you continue reading "Chef Huey," underline or circle parts of the text that raise questions. Write your questions in the **Response Notes**.

from Chef Huey *continued*

The chef with the biggest smile of all was Chef Marco on the can of Chef Marco's Spaghetti.

"Please get that can," I said to my mom. "I want to take it home."

I wanted to invent something with it, but I wasn't sure what.

At first I couldn't think of anything it went with. Instead, I thought of cakes like pillows. I thought of carrots that would be fastened together around meat loaf to make skyscrapers. One night I did tie some carrots around a meat loaf my dad made—but the strings that fastened them came loose in the oven, and the skyscraper fell down.

It was the night before Mother's Day when I thought of a brand-new food.

I could see it in my mind. <u>Something yellow. A happy yellow food.</u> One that didn't mind being eaten.

Response Notes

Will he make a
lemon food?

DETERMINING IMPORTANCE

As you read, you pause at times to **determine which details and ideas are important.** You use your background knowledge, opinions, and purpose for reading to help you make your choices. Your choices may be different from someone else's.

As you read the next part of "Chef Huey," notice the details the author includes about Huey's idea. Underline the most important sentences, phrases, and words. Explain your choices in the **Response Notes**.

Huey wants to mix bananas and spaghetti!

from Chef Huey continued

In the morning, Julian and I were going to bring my mom breakfast in bed. Julian was going to fry eggs. I told him I had a better idea.

"What is it?" he asked.

"Banana Spaghetti," I said.

"Banana Spaghetti!" he said. "I never heard of it!"

"It's a new invention!" I said. "It will be a one hundred percent surprise."

Julian likes surprises. "So how do we make it?" he asked.

"Simple!" I said. "We have bananas and we have spaghetti. All we have to do is put them together."

Julian thought about it. "We'd better get up early tomorrow," he said. "Just in case."

When you read, certain words and phrases help you **visualize**, or create images in your mind. Words or phrases that appeal to your five senses—sight, sound, taste, touch, feel—help you visualize images from a text. Visualizing helps you better connect with and understand what you're reading.

As you read the next passage from "Chef Huey," underline words and phrases that spark images in your mind. In the **Response Notes**, write about or draw the images you see and feel while reading.

from Chef Huey *continued*

At 6 A.M. we went downstairs very quietly and turned on the lights in the kitchen. We went to work.

We mashed up three ripe bananas. I took out the can of Chef Marco's Spaghetti. In the picture on the can, Chef Marco had his arms spread out wide, with a steaming platter balanced above his head on one hand.

I decided to stand that way when I brought Mom the Banana Spaghetti. I would go up the stairs ahead of Julian with her plate, so Julian couldn't take all the credit.

Response Notes

I imagine messy, slimy bananas in a bowl.

MAKING INFERENCES

Authors don't include every possible detail when they write. They purposely leave out bits of information that they expect you to **infer**, or figure out. In a text, look for clues that reveal hidden details the author doesn't state. When you fill in the gaps with your own thoughts, you are **making an inference**. An inference can be a conclusion or a prediction. Making inferences will deepen your understanding of a text.

As you read the next section of "Chey Huey," infer what you think will happen next. Underline sentences and phrases that spark your inferences. Write your inferences in the **Response Notes**.

Response Notes

It's going to taste horrible!

from Chef Huey *continued*

I held the can and Julian opened it. We put the spaghetti in a bowl. It had a lot of tomato sauce on it—the color of blood.

"We have to get the tomato off!" I said.

We put the spaghetti in the sink and washed it with hot water. It got nice and clean. We put it on a platter.

"It looks kind of spongy," Julian said.

"It will be good," I said. "We just need to put the sauce on it."

Julian dumped all the mashed banana on the top.

"Banana Spaghetti!" I said.

"Taste it!" Julian said.

<u>But I wasn't sure I wanted to.</u>

"You try it!" I said.

As you read and reread a text, your thoughts and ideas change. You learn new information that affects how you think or feel about a piece. As your thoughts and ideas evolve, you **synthesize**, or create, new understandings. Often these new understandings are big ideas or themes the author is trying to get across.

When you finish "Chef Huey," reread the Response Notes for the entire selection. Think about the twists and turns your mind took along the way. Then review all your thoughts and feelings about the piece to synthesize some big ideas or themes. Write your big ideas or themes in the **Response Notes**.

from Chef Huey continued

Julian tasted it. His lips puckered up. He wiped his mouth with a kitchen towel.

"It will be better when it's hot," he said.

We put it in a pan on the stove and it got hot. Very hot. The banana scorched. It smelled like burning rubber.

Julian turned off the stove. We looked into the pan.

"Not all of it burned," Julian said. "Just the bottom. We can put the rest on the plates."

We did. Then we looked at it.

Banana Spaghetti was not the way I had imagined it. It wasn't yellow. It was brown. It wasn't happy. It looked miserable.

It looked worse than turnips, worse than eggplant, worse than a baked fish eye. ✦

Response Notes

Inventing a new food might not always work.

Making Connections

Imagine that you are reading a book. The main character begs his mother for a dog. You say to yourself, "I tried that, but it didn't work." You have just made a connection. You compared something you read with your own experience. **Making connections** will help you better understand what you read. The connections will bring you closer to the characters and ideas in a selection.

In this unit, you will practice making connections with people, thoughts, and ideas. All the people you will read about are **following their dreams.** See if you can find the dream in each selection.

Think about the Dr. Seuss books you know. Two well-known titles are *Green Eggs and Ham* and *The Cat in the Hat*. Do you know that Dr. Seuss was a real person? He was born in 1904 in Massachusetts. This selection will tell you a little about his childhood.

As you read, think about how you and Dr. Seuss are alike and different. Underline details that tell you what Dr. Seuss liked to do as a child. In the **Response Notes**, write any connections you make with his experiences. An example has been done for you. If a detail reminds you of something, that's a connection.

Response Notes

I like books and animals, too.

I wish I could try sledding.

from The Boy on Fairfield Street
by Kathleen Krull

Once upon a time, there lived a boy who feasted on books and was wild about animals.

He was born in 1904 and lived in the best of all possible places—74 Fairfield Street in Springfield, Massachusetts. The gray three-story house was exactly three blocks from the public library. And it was just six blocks from the zoo.

This boy loved lots of things besides reading and animals—sledding, doodling, trying on costumes, singing around the piano with his family, exploring the green fields of nearby Forest Park. All in all, he excelled at fooling around.

No one on Fairfield Street could have said how Ted Geisel, that funny boy, would turn out.

No one in the world could have.

Especially Ted.

At dinner, Ted's family gathered around the huge oak table. Often they talked about the animals in the zoo.

Ted's father, Theodor Geisel, worked in the family business. But he also helped out at the zoo and eventually was superintendent of parks—which meant he actually *ran* the zoo. Ted would eat baked beans and bratwurst and thrill to stories of stubborn bears and chattering monkeys, prowling lions and wild wolves.

At night, their hoots and cries sometimes found their way into his dreams.

Ted's mother, Henrietta Seuss Geisel, helped him find books at the library. Her dream was to get Ted and his sister, Marnie, into college, as the first in their family to go. Perhaps Ted might even grow up to become "Dr. Geisel."

Each night she lulled them to sleep with stories and nonsense verse, like the names of pies: "Apple, mince, lemon . . . peach, apricot, pineapple . . . blueberry, coconut, custard, and SQUASH!"

Ted would listen, curled up with a gift from her— his first stuffed animal, a plump dog he had named Theophrastus. ❖

ZOO

ZOO

✳ In this selection, you learn about what Dr. Seuss liked to do as a boy. His interests are shown in the chart below. Place a check next to those you like to do, too.

Likes	Dr. Seuss as a boy	Me
Reading	X	
Animals	X	
Sledding	X	
Doodling	X	
Trying on costumes	X	
Singing	X	
Exploring fields	X	
Fooling around	X	

✳ Do you have interests that are not on Dr. Seuss's list? Write them below.

Activities I like to do:

1. ....

2. ....

3. ....

4. ....

✳ Use the two charts on page 18 to write a summary about how you and Dr. Seuss are alike and different. The first paragraph can tell how the two of you are alike. The second paragraph can tell how the two of you are different.

Making connections with a person will help you better understand the person.

Everyone has hopes and dreams. But what's the best way to make them happen? This selection will show you how one person followed his dream.

Benny Goodman was a famous musician who was born around the same time as Dr. Seuss. As you read about Benny's childhood, underline details that show his hopes and dreams. Write your connections with them in the **Response Notes**.

from Once Upon a Time in Chicago
by Jonah Winter

Benny was a quiet boy. Benny never had too much to say. He smiled politely a lot. He was the shyest kid in his fourth-grade class. But when Benny got home and opened up his clarinet case, his eyes sparkled. The clarinet case was lined with purple velvet. The clarinet itself was black and shiny with silver keys. What an instrument!

<u>Benny liked playing the clarinet more than he liked talking.</u> For a while, Benny's family couldn't keep him away from his instrument. His brothers and sisters made him practice on the fire escape.

His practice paid off. Before long, he was in a marching band. Benny's father was thrilled. He hoped Benny could grow up to make more money and have a better life.

Though he could scarcely afford it, David Goodman signed Benny up for some lessons with the great Franz Schoepp.

Benny practiced and practiced and practiced— scales, whole tones, and exercises from books. Franz Schoepp was training Benny to become a classical clarinetist, like himself.

My sister plays the clarinet, but she doesn't like to practice.

But Benny loved a new kind of music called jazz. Jazz was fun and hot, and it made people want to get up and dance. Benny listened to his brothers' jazz records on a phonograph. He memorized the clarinet solos note for note.

Benny heard about an "Amateur Night" at the Central Park Theater in downtown Chicago. People performed different acts. Benny brought his clarinet.

When he got up on stage, in front of a huge audience, Benny wasn't even nervous. He played his solos he had memorized. His tunes were a big hit!

A week later the phone rang. It was the theater owner. He asked Benny if he could fill in for someone that night.

Benny was there in a flash. In one hour, he made five dollars. It was more than his father made in a whole day.

Word got out about Benny. He got a call from a nightclub where a jazz band played. When he arrived, the bandleader asked if Benny could play a difficult song.

Not only could Benny play it—he played it sixteen times in sixteen different keys, without stopping! And it was beautiful. Everyone wanted to know: Who was this kid? ✦

1. He practiced on the fire escape.

2.

3.

4.

✳ Words that describe people are called character traits. List two or three character traits that helped Benny work toward his dream.

1. ....

2. ....

3. ....

✳ Do you or someone you know have any of these traits? Explain.

....

....

....

....

✳ Benny surprised others with his musical talent. Write about one of your talents and why it might surprise others, too.

....

....

....

....

....

....

✳ **What dreams do you have for yourself? Pick your favorite and explain how you will reach it.**

....

....

....

....

....

....

✳ **How does making connections with a person help you better understand that person?**

....

....

....

....

....

....

Making connections with another person's dreams can help you better understand the person. It can also help you figure out your own dreams.

When you **make connections** with a person's actions, you will better understand and remember the person. In this selection, you will read about Tomie dePaola's actions in kindergarten. Tomie dePaola is a famous children's writer. You may have read some of his books, such as *Strega Nona* and *Charlie Needs a Cloak*.

As you read about Tomie's first day in kindergarten, underline details that show his actions and decisions. In the **Response Notes**, write about any connections you make.

from 26 Fairmount Avenue
by Tomie dePaola

The room was filled with kids crying and hanging onto their mothers. *Boy*, I thought, *what babies*. I didn't realize that I would be in school with those kids for years and years.

I went up to a lady who looked like she might be the teacher. She was.

"And who are we?" she asked. (She always used "we." "We must take our naps now," or "We must bring our chairs into a circle"—stuff like that.)

"I'm Tomie dePaola," I said.

"Oh, aren't we lucky," she said. "I had your big brother, Joseph, in kindergarten, too," (she was talking about Buddy). Well, I figured it wouldn't take too long for her to realize that my brother and I were *very* different. But that could wait.

"When do we learn how to read?" I asked.

"Oh, we don't learn how to read in kindergarten. We learn to read next year, in first grade."

"Fine," I said. "I'll be back next year." And I walked right out of the school and all the way home.

Response Notes

No one was there. My dad was working at the barbershop, and my mom was off shopping all by herself for the first time in a long while.

The school called my dad at the barbershop. He found my mom, and they came roaring home to Columbus Avenue.

There I was, holding one of my mom's big books, staring at it, hoping that I could learn to read by myself.

When I told Mom and Dad what had happened, my dad said, "You handle this one, Floss." And he went back to work.

My mom sat down next to me. "You know," she said, "if you don't go to kindergarten, you won't pass. And if you don't pass, you'll never get into first grade, and you'll never learn to read."

So I went back to school, but I never really liked kindergarten. ✦

✳ **What is one important reason that explains why Tomie didn't like kindergarten? Write about it.**

....

....

....

....

....

....

✳ **Think about Tomie's actions. Write about one of them and what you think this tells you about Tomie as a child.**

....

....

....

....

....

✳ **What's another way Tomie could have resolved his problem, instead of leaving school?**

✳ **Tell about your favorite grade so far in school and why it's your favorite.**

Making connections with a person's actions and decisions can help you better understand the person.

4 LESSON

Poems often include strong images, or the pictures you see in your mind. Which poem speaks to you more? What images do you see in your mind?

As you read the poems, underline words or phrases that create images in your mind. In the **Response Notes**, write about the connections you make.

Basketball Star by Karama Fufuka

When I get big
I want to be the best
basketball player in the world.
I'll make jumpshots, hookballs
and layups
and talk about dribble—
mine'll be outta sight!

Response Notes

Growing Up by Harry Behn

When I was seven
We went for a picnic
Up to a magic
Foresty place.
I knew there were tigers
Behind every boulder,
Though I didn't meet one
Face to face.

When I was older
We went for a picnic
Up to the very same
Place as before,
And all of the trees
And the rocks were so little
They couldn't hide tigers
Or *me* anymore. ✣

❋ **How did the author change as he got older? Explain.**

* The poem "Growing Up" has two stanzas. Draw a picture that goes with the first stanza. Then draw a picture that goes with the second stanza. Before you begin, think about how the two pictures will be different.

✳ The poem "Growing Up" talks about how thoughts, feelings, and dreams can change as you get older. What were some of your thoughts, feelings, or dreams when you were younger? How have they changed over time? Write them below.

My thoughts, feelings, or dreams when I was younger:

My thoughts, feelings, or dreams now:

✳ Look back through the selections in this unit. Which person did you connect with the most? Why?

Connecting with images in a poem will help you better understand the poem.

Asking Questions

Suppose your teacher tells you that you're going on a field trip. You'd probably ask: Where are we going? When are we going? How will we get there? What will we do there? Asking questions is a great way to get information.

When you read, you can ask questions, too. **Asking questions** will help you figure out what you already know and what you would like to know. It will also help you stay interested in your reading as you search for the answers.

All the selections in this unit are about people who make **change** in their lives and in the lives of others. As you read, you will practice asking questions to better understand the selections.

BOISTEROUS

What if someone described you as *boisterous*? Would you agree or disagree? Would you like being described by that word, or not?

In this selection from the short novel *Donavan's Word Jar*, Donavan discovers that **one word can make a big difference** in how a person feels about him- or herself. As you read, look for and underline the special words that cause the characters to think about how they feel about themselves. In the **Response Notes**, write questions or thoughts you have about the words or the story.

Response Notes

from Donavan's Word Jar
by Monalisa DeGross

Donavan waited while Grandma got her coat and locked her apartment door. She was carrying a big brown paper sack, and he wondered what was in it. As they walked down the hall, Donavan began to tell Grandma about how he had helped Miz Marylou and Mr. Bill Gut.

When Grandma and Donavan got to the lounge, Donavan could not believe what he saw. Grandma's neighbors were up and around, laughing and talking. They all seemed excited. He looked around to see what was going on. Donavan saw that they were waving little yellow slips of paper in their hands.

"MY WORDS! THEY HAVE MY WORDS!" Donavan shouted.

Some people had one slip of paper in their hands, others had two. Mr. Avery was no longer slumped in front of the TV. He was tacking one of Donavan's words up on the bulletin board. Miss Millie was looking up the word on her slip of paper in a pocket dictionary. Donavan looked over at the desk and saw

Why are
Donavan's words
in the lounge?

Mrs. Agnes digging into his word jar. There were people in a line behind her laughing and talking. They were waiting to get a word from his jar.

"WHAT'S GOING ON?" Donavan asked, as loud as he could. "GRANDMA! STOP THEM. THEY ARE TAKING MY WORDS!" He turned to his grandma, but she looked just as surprised as he felt.

"Donnie, calm down. They didn't know. You left the jar on the desk," she said in a quiet voice.

"I AM GOING TO GET MY WORD JAR," Donavan said firmly. "EXCUSE ME," he shouted. "EXCUSE ME, MAY I GET PAST?" he yelled, moving through the crowd. He pushed a little, he even shoved a bit. It was no use. Donavan couldn't stop what was happening.

Mr. Crawford, the mailman, passed Donavan and waved his word over his head. "PERSEVERANCE," he called out. "That's just the word I need. Some days I get so tired, I can hardly make it. I'm going to try just a little harder to keep going," he said, tucking the word in his shirt pocket.

Donavan stopped pushing and stood still.

"Wow! One of my words made Mr. Crawford feel better," Donavan said. He looked around and saw Miss Millie talking to Mr. Foote. Donavan was surprised.

"BOISTEROUS," he heard Miss Millie say in her soft voice. Grandma always told Donavan that Miss Millie was so shy that she hardly ever spoke to anyone.

Mr. Foote, on the other hand, spoke to everyone.

I think this word means "sticking to something," or not giving up. I've heard the soccer coach use that word.

TIMID

BOISTEROUS

PERSEVERANCE

"Well, I'll be darned," Mr. Foote said in surprise. "My word is "TIMID!"

"Perhaps we should exchange words," Miss Millie suggested.

"Oh, no. Maybe I need to quiet down some. Sometimes I am a bit loud," Mr. Foote said softly.

"You're right, I think I'll keep my word too. I am going to start speaking to people more. I am going to change my ways." Miss Millie's voice sounded like she meant it.

"Did my words do that, make them want to change?" Donavan asked himself in surprise.

All around him, Grandma's neighbors were laughing and talking to each other. They had never acted so lively before. ✦

✳ How do the words from Donavan's word jar affect the characters? Write your thoughts in the boxes below.

Mr. Crawford's word: *perseverance*
How does this word affect him?

It made him realize that he could try harder to keep going.

Miss Millie's word:
How does this word affect her?

Mr. Foote's word:
How does this word affect him?

✳ **How do Donavan's actions cause change?**

✳ **Choose three words that you would use to describe yourself.**

1. ....

2. ....

3. ....

✳ **Now choose three words that a friend or family member might use to describe you.**

1. ....

2. ....

3. ....

✳ **If the words are different or the same, explain why.**

....

....

....

....

....

....

....

Asking questions about words in a story will help you better understand the story.

A **tradition** is a custom that has been passed down from generation to generation. Traditions can help you connect with the past. What traditions do you know about? How have they changed over time?

As you read the poem called "Tradition," notice the questions you have before, during, and after you read. Write your questions on page 40. How do your questions change before, during, and after you read? In the **Response Notes**, jot down notes you want to remember.

Tradition by Eloise Greenfield

Pineapples! pumpkins! chickens! we
carry them on our heads you see
we can glide along forever
and not drop a thing, no never
never even use our hands
never put a finger to it
you know how we learned to do it?
knowledge came from other lands
Africans of long ago
passed it down to us and so
now we pass it on to you
for what is old is also new
pineapples, pumpkins, chickens, we
carry more than the things you see
we also carry history ✣

Response
Notes

✳ **How did your questions change before, during, and after you read the poem?**

My questions before reading:

What will this poem be about?

My questions during reading:

My questions after reading:

✳ **What do you think the author means by "for what is old is also new"?**

....

....

....

....

....

....

✳ **How can a tradition teach you about history?**

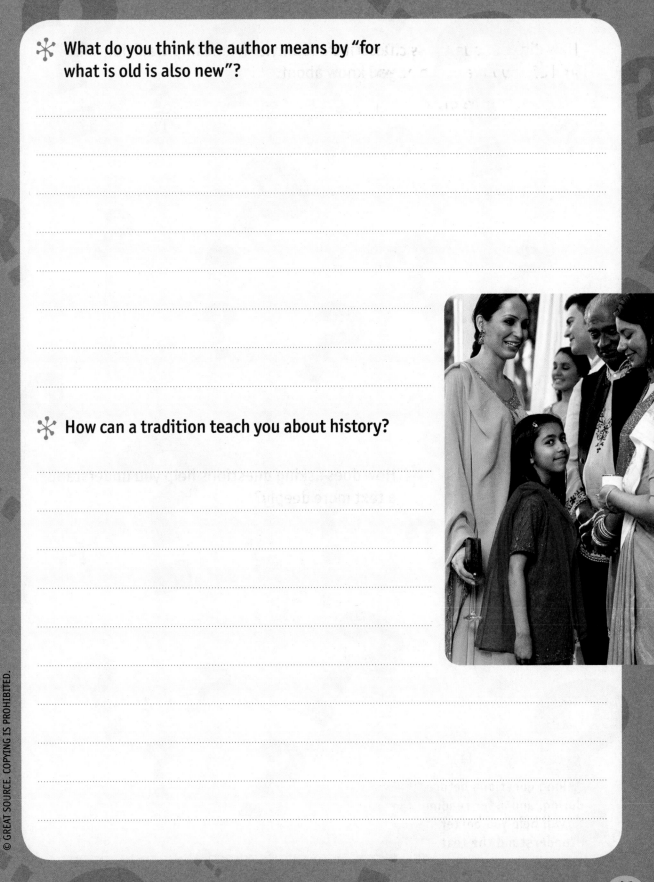

....

....

....

....

....

....

....

....

✳ **Describe a family or friendship tradition that you know about.**

....

....

....

....

....

....

....

✳ **How does asking questions help you understand a text more deeply?**

....

....

....

....

....

....

Asking questions before, during, and after reading will help you better understand the text.

3 LESSON

Reading is a little like taking a walk. As you walk, you mostly look ahead to watch where you're going. But you also look around to notice the scenery. Sometimes you even stop to look at something more carefully.

When you read, your mind works to create a big picture. Often, you'll notice details that make you stop and wonder. **Asking questions** about these details will help you create a big picture that makes sense.

This excerpt is from a fiction book called *The Printer*. The narrator's father, who is deaf, notices a fire at work. As you read about the fire, think carefully about the events. Underline details that raise questions. Write your questions in the **Response Notes**.

from The Printer by Myron Uhlberg

Sometimes my father felt sad about the way he was treated by his fellow workers who could hear. <u>Because they couldn't talk to him with their hands,</u> they seemed to ignore him. Years went by as my father and the hearing printers worked side by side. They never once exchanged a single thought.

But my father did not lack friends. There were other printers at the plant who were deaf. They had also learned to talk with their hands.

One day, while the giant presses ran, their noises shutting out all other sound, my father spotted a fire flickering in a far corner of the pressroom.

The fire was spreading quickly, silently. Suddenly, the wood floor burst into flames.

My father knew he had to tell everyone. He couldn't speak to shout a warning. Even if he could, no one would hear him over the loud roar of the presses.

Response Notes

Is the author talking about sign language?

But he could speak with his hands.

He did not hesitate. He jumped onto an ink drum and waved his arms excitedly until, clear across the room, he caught the attention of a fellow printer who also couldn't hear a sound.

My father's hands shouted through the terrible noise of the printing presses,

FIRE! FIRE!
TELL EVERYONE TO GET OUT!
TELL THE HEARING ONES!

His friend climbed onto a huge roll of newsprint. His fingers screamed to the other deaf workers,

FIRE! FIRE!
TELL THE HEARING ONES!

All the printers who couldn't hear ran to fellow workers who could. They pointed to the fire, which had now spread to the wall next to the only exit.

Not one of my father's friends left until everyone knew of the danger. My father was the last to escape. ❖

✳ Look over your Response Notes. Choose one question you wrote. Talk about it with a partner. What answers did you find together? Write them below.

Question:

....

....

....

....

Answers:

....

....

....

✳ Do you think the father is a hero? Give reasons to support your answer.

....

....

....

....

....

....

....

....

....

✳ **Write a letter that a hearing printer might write to the father. How do you think the hearing printer feels? How might his feelings about the author's father have changed because of the fire? Include this in the letter.**

Date: ....

Dear .... , ...

....

....

....

....

....

....

....

....

....

Signed, ...

....

Asking questions while reading can help you figure out what the author wants you to understand.

Disasters, such as floods and fires, can change people's lives dramatically. As you read the second half of *The Printer*, think about how all the characters' lives might have changed because of the fire. **Asking questions** about these changes will help you better understand the story.

As you read, underline words or phrases that show or hint of changes in the characters' lives. In the **Response Notes**, write questions about the changes.

from The Printer by Myron Uhlberg

By the time everyone had fled, the fire—feeding on huge quantities of paper—had engulfed the enormous plant. The giant presses, some still spewing out burning sheets of newspaper, had fallen partly through the floor. Great shafts of flame shot out of the bursting windows.

The printers stood in the street, broken glass at their feet. They embraced one another as the fire engines arrived. They were happy to be alive.

My father stood alone, struck numb by the last image of the burning presses.

The fire destroyed the printing presses. The plant had to close for repairs. But not one printer had been hurt.

When the printing plant finally reopened, my father went back to the work he loved. The new presses were switched on and roared into life.

Response Notes

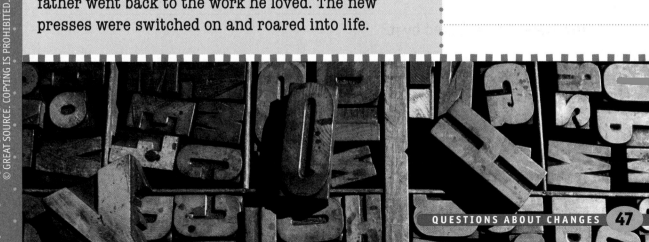

When the day's newspaper had been printed, the presses shuddered to a stop. Now there was silence.

In the midst of the stillness, my father's co-workers gathered around him. They presented him with a hat made of the freshly printed newspaper.

And as my father put the hat on his head, all the printers who could hear did something surprising. They told him THANK YOU with their hands. ❖

✳ Write about two important changes that happened because of the fire. Who was affected by the changes? How were they affected? Write your thoughts in the two charts.

What is one change?
Who was affected by it?
How were they affected by it?

What is another change?

Who was affected by it?

How were they affected by it?

✳ **Why do you think the father stood alone as he watched the fire?**

✳ Plan and write a news story about the fire. Use the 5Ws to plan the story. Then write the story on the next page.

5WS PLANNING CHART FOR A NEWS STORY

What happened?	
Where did it happen?	
When did it happen?	
Why did it happen?	
Who was involved?	

✳ **Write your news story here. Include specific details. Create a headline that hooks your readers.**

NEWS

✳ **Discuss these two questions with a partner:**

■ How does asking questions help you remember the details of a selection?

■ How does asking questions help you better understand the whole selection?

Write the most important points you discussed.

....

....

....

....

....

....

....

....

....

....

....

....

Asking questions about changes in a story will help you better understand what the changes mean.

Determining Importance

Suppose your baseball coach asks, "What is the most important thing I should know about you?" You might say, "I want to be a pitcher." What if your piano teacher asks you the same question. Your answer might be different.

When you read, you are asking the same kind of question to the words on the page: *What are your most important ideas?* It depends on your purpose for reading and your beliefs and opinions.

In this unit, you will practice **determining the importance of ideas** in a selection. You will become aware of why you think certain ideas are more important than others. Each selection in this unit is about **maintaining balance**—in people's lives and in the natural world.

I f you want to learn about the earth, would you rather read a book or a rock? Rocks don't have words, of course, but they can still give you lots of information if you know how to examine them.

As you read this nonfiction article about rocks, underline details that give you information. In the **Response Notes**, write the details you think are the most important, and why. Noticing and thinking about details will help you figure out the most important ideas in a selection.

Response Notes

from **Rock Secrets** by Betsy James

A rock is never just a rock.
A rock is a mystery.

Pick up a rock. Any rock. Does it look as if it has a secret?

Because it does. A big one. As big as a volcano. Or an ocean. Or a ferocious dinosaur. Every rock has a secret story to tell about what the earth was like long ago.

Could where you're sitting this very second once have been a pool of lava? Or the bottom of an ocean? Or a tropical forest?

Maybe. How can you tell?

You pick up a rock.

Is your rock sandy or gritty? It's probably sandstone. To make sandstone, millions of years of wind and rain wore down mountains until nothing was left but grains of sand. That sand made deserts and beaches; in time it stuck together and became rock. Sandstone sometimes shows ripples left by long-ago winds or waves.

This is important because sandstone can tell you about old mountains that don't exist anymore.

Did you pick up a piece of shiny black obsidian? It came out of a volcano! When a volcano erupts, some lava may cool so fast that it hardens into this smooth, glassy rock.

Does your rock have sparkly crystals? Then it once spent time far underground, where heat from deeply buried lava, called magma, can help crystals grow. If you look at the very hard rock called granite, you'll see the different colors of many mineral crystals.

If you're *really* lucky, you might pick up a piece of dinosaur bone. How can a scientist tell if the rock she picks up is a dinosaur fossil? She might touch her tongue to it. If it's bone, tiny holes where blood vessels once ran will usually make her tongue stick a little.

Or you might find a gastrolith, a round, smooth, shiny stone that once spent time in a dinosaur's stomach, helping it grind up its dinner of plants.

Does every rock have a secret story?

Yes, every single rock—even a tiny pebble from your playground. It won't tell you its story in words. You have to figure it out by looking, feeling, asking, and wondering. But first—Pick up a rock! ❖

✳ Look over the details you noticed. What do you think are the two most important ideas in the article? Why?

Important idea	Why is it important?

Name of rock	Characteristics (looks like, feels like)	How is it formed?
obsidian		
fossil		

✳ The earth has changed over time. How does studying rocks help you understand this big idea?

....

....

....

....

....

....

....

Thinking about the details in a selection will help you find the big ideas.

2 LESSON

You can learn a lot about the natural world by studying the **relationships** in it. The natural world maintains its balance through many different relationships.

In this nonfiction article, you'll read about an unusual spider. As you read, underline the details that show the spider's relationship with the natural world. In the **Response Notes**, write what's important about the relationship.

from **Real Live Monsters!**
by Ellen Schecter

GIANT BIRD-EATING SPIDER
(Theraphosa leblondi)
Surinam

MEET THE MONSTER SPIDER:
the largest in the world! Its body is nearly 4 inches long. Its leg span is up to 11 inches wide! It weighs almost as much as a quarter-pounder from McDonald's!

When it gets scared, this giant makes a purring noise. It rises up on its fourth pair of legs to look even larger! Its bite hurts, but isn't poisonous to humans.

This giant eats insects, small lizards, and small snakes (even poisonous ones). It also catches and eats small birds!

In 1705, Maria Merian published a book of paintings she did in the Amazon jungle. One shows a huge spider dragging a hummingbird from its nest. Nobody believed her for **158 years . . . when another scientist** finally *saw these spiders killing small birds.*

Response Notes

It tries to scare away its predators.

This giant stabs its prey with poison fangs up to one inch long. Its venom turns the inside of its victim's body to liquid. Then it sips up the insides.

What do **you** think: **M-M-M-MONSTER**? Or just eating to live? ❖

❋ Write or draw a timeline of the spider catching, killing, and eating its prey.

Catching prey	Killing prey	Eating prey

❋ What important ideas does this selection tell you about the relationship between this spider and the natural world?

✳ How does the giant bird-eating spider help the natural world maintain balance?

✳ How does thinking about details help you figure out the important ideas in a selection?

Studying relationships in nature can help you figure out important ideas about the natural world.

A poem often has fewer words than a story. But a poem can still tell a story. A poet paints **images**, or pictures, with words. He or she wants the readers to "see" the pictures in their mind.

As you read the poem, notice the pictures you see in your mind. How do the pictures lead you to the most important ideas in the poem? As you read, underline words and phrases that create images in your mind. In the **Response Notes**, write about what the images tell you.

In Hong Kong by Kam Mak

Response Notes

In Hong Kong, my grandmother
is in her kitchen
making pickled kumquats.

In Chinatown, there are kumquats
piled high on every street cart,
wooden crates packed full of suns.
Mama takes forever, hunting for
the ones with leaves attached.
Leaves are good luck.

But she doesn't know how to pickle them.
Grandmother wouldn't tell her.
"If I told you, you'd never come to see me again!"
she said, and winked,
slipping one last kumquat
into my bowl. ✢

✳ Which images in the poem do you think are the most important? Why?

Description of image	What does this image tell you?

✳ What does the author mean when she writes "wooden crates packed full of suns"? Why do you think she chose those words?

....

....

....

....

....

....

✳ Why do you think Grandmother winks at the narrator, near the end of the poem?

✳ How does this poem connect to the idea of maintaining balance?

※ **What special foods are eaten in your family? Do you have a relative or friend who likes to cook a special dish? Explain.**

Thinking about the images in a poem will lead you to the important ideas in the poem.

When people communicate with each other, they **interact.** In stories, the **interactions** between characters can give you a lot of information about them.

In this passage from the short novel *Sarah, Plain and Tall*, Anna and Caleb's father has put an ad in the paper, looking for a new wife. Their mother died when Caleb was a baby.

As you read, underline sentences that show when characters interact. In the **Response Notes**, write what you feel is important about the interactions.

Response Notes

Their laughing together means they agree..

from Sarah, Plain and Tall
by Patricia MacLachlan

Papa might not have told us about Sarah that night if Caleb hadn't asked him the question. After the dishes were cleared and washed and Papa was filling the tin pail with ashes, Caleb spoke up. It wasn't a question, really.

"You don't sing anymore," he said. He said it harshly. Not because he meant to, but because he had been thinking of it for so long. "Why?" he asked more gently.

Slowly Papa straightened up. There was a long silence, and the dogs looked up, wondering at it.

"I've forgotten the old songs," said Papa quietly. He sat down. "But maybe there's a way to remember them." He looked up at us.

"How?" asked Caleb eagerly.

Papa leaned back in the chair. "I've placed an advertisement in the newspapers. For help."

"You mean a housekeeper?" I asked, surprised.

Caleb and I looked at each other and burst out laughing, remembering Hilly, our old housekeeper.

She was round and slow and shuffling. She snored in a high whistle at night, like a teakettle, and let the fire go out.

"No," said Papa slowly. "Not a housekeeper." He paused. "A wife."

Caleb stared at Papa. "A wife? You mean a mother?"

Nick [the dog] slid his face onto Papa's lap and Papa stroked his ears.

"That, too," said Papa. "Like Maggie."

Matthew, our neighbor to the south, had written to ask for a wife and mother for his children. And Maggie had come from Tennessee. Her hair was the color of turnips and she laughed.

Papa reached into his pocket and unfolded a letter written on white paper. "And I have received an answer." Papa read to us:

Dear Mr. Jacob Witting,

I am Sarah Wheaton from Maine as you will see from my letter. I am answering your advertisement. I have never been married, though I have been asked. I have lived with an older brother, William, who is about to be married. His wife-to-be is young and energetic.

I have always loved to live by the sea, but at this time I feel a move is necessary. And the truth is, the sea is as far east as I can go. My choice, as you can see, is limited. This should not be taken as an insult. I am strong and I work hard and I am willing to travel. But I am not mild mannered. If you should still care to write, I would be interested in your children and about where you live. And you.

Very truly yours,
Sarah Elisabeth Wheaton

P.S. Do you have opinions on cats? I have one.

No one spoke when Papa finished the letter. He kept looking at it in his hands, reading it over to himself. Finally I turned my head a bit to sneak a look at Caleb. He was smiling. I smiled, too. ❖

✳ Look over the selection and your Response Notes. What important ideas do the characters' interactions tell you about their lives?

✳ Why do you think Caleb and Anna were smiling after Papa read the letter?

✳ **How is Papa's letter connected to the theme of maintaining balance?**

....

....

....

....

....

....

....

....

✳ With a partner, discuss how thinking about important ideas helped you better understand the selections in this unit. Then complete the chart.

Selection title	What I understood better by thinking about the important ideas
Rock Secrets 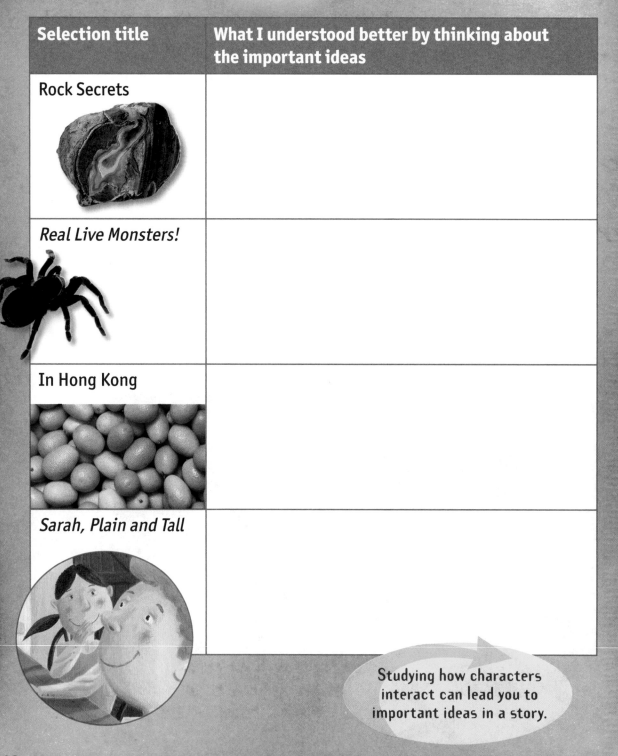	
Real Live Monsters!	
In Hong Kong	
Sarah, Plain and Tall	

Studying how characters interact can lead you to important ideas in a story.

Visualizing

Think about eating a big, juicy strawberry. What does it look like? What does it taste like? What does it smell like? When you imagine answers to these questions, you are **visualizing**. You are using your senses of taste, smell, sight, sound, and touch to create a detailed picture in your mind.

When you read, you can visualize, too. Creating pictures in your mind of the details you read will help you better understand, remember, and enjoy the text.

In this unit, you will practice creating pictures in your mind. All the selections relate to the theme of **differences**—in people's lives and in the natural world.

Sometimes a map or graph is the best way for an author to give readers information. Maps and graphs give information in pictures.

This nonfiction passage is about places that hold world records. As you read, try to imagine the details that the maps and graphs show you. In the **Response Notes**, write thoughts or questions about the details.

Response Notes

How long would it take to travel down the Nile?

from **Hottest, Coldest, Highest, Deepest** by Steve Jenkins

The Nile, in Africa, is the longest river in the world. It is 4,145 miles long.

Nile River (4,145 miles)

Amazon River (4,007 miles)

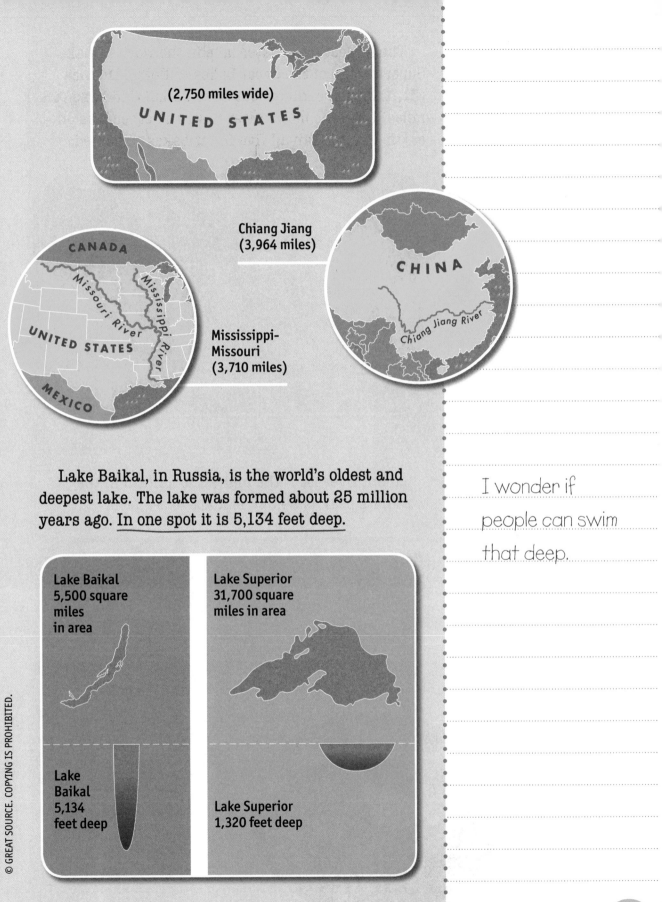

(2,750 miles wide)

UNITED STATES

Chiang Jiang
(3,964 miles)

CHINA

CANADA

Missouri River

Mississippi River

UNITED STATES

MEXICO

Chiang Jiang River

Mississippi-
Missouri
(3,710 miles)

Lake Baikal, in Russia, is the world's oldest and deepest lake. The lake was formed about 25 million years ago. In one spot it is 5,134 feet deep.

I wonder if people can swim that deep.

Lake Baikal
5,500 square
miles
in area

Lake Superior
31,700 square
miles in area

Lake
Baikal
5,134
feet deep

Lake Superior
1,320 feet deep

The largest freshwater lake in the world is Lake Superior, one of the Great Lakes in North America (31,700 square miles), but Lake Baikal (5,500 square miles) contains more water than any other lake on earth—more than all five Great Lakes combined.

Mount Everest is the highest mountain in the world. Its peak is 29,028 feet above sea level.

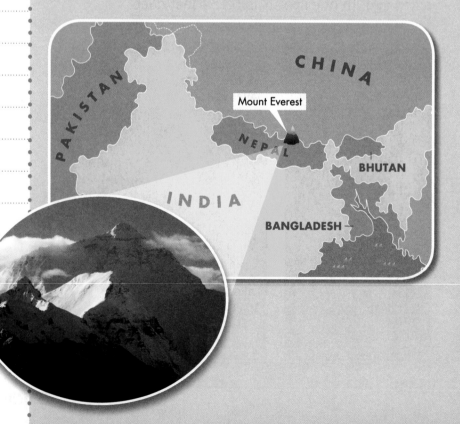

The hottest temperature ever recorded in the
United States is 134.6° F, in Death Valley, California.

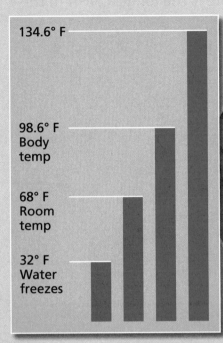

134.6° F

98.6° F
Body
temp

68° F
Room
temp

32° F
Water
freezes

The coldest place on the planet is Vostok,
Antarctica. A temperature of 129° F below zero was
recorded there. ✤

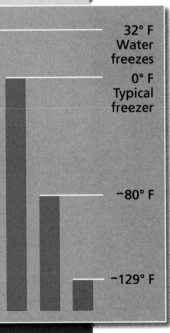

32° F
Water
freezes

0° F
Typical
freezer

−80° F

−129° F

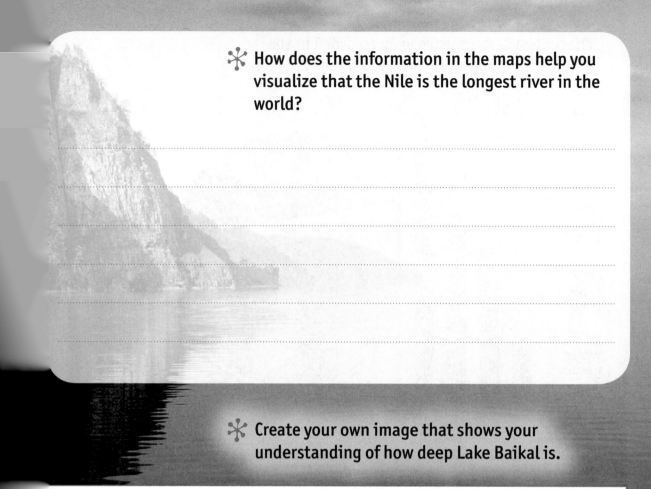

✳ How does the information in the maps help you visualize that the Nile is the longest river in the world?

_____

_____

_____

_____

_____

_____

✳ Create your own image that shows your understanding of how deep Lake Baikal is.

✳ **Tell about the hottest or coldest place you have ever visited.**

....

....

....

....

....

....

✳ **Create a map or graph that shows some information about the place you described above.**

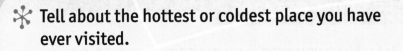

Use charts and maps to help you picture information.

When you read, you are sometimes able to **visualize,** or create a picture in your mind, from just one word. Other times, a phrase or sentence will help you. Visualizing will help you better understand and remember what you read.

In this nonfiction passage, the author writes about what children of different cultures do when they lose a tooth. As you read, underline words, phrases, or sentences that create pictures in your mind. In the **Response Notes**, draw or write about the pictures you see.

Response Notes

from **Throw Your Tooth on the Roof** by Selby B. Beeler

Cameroon
I throw my tooth over the roof, shouting, "Take this bad tooth and bring me a new one." Then I hop around my house on one foot and everyone laughs.

Botswana
I throw my tooth on the roof and say, "Mr. Moon, Mr. Moon, please bring me a new tooth."

Mali
I throw my tooth in the chicken coop. <u>The next day I might find a big fat hen in the coop and my mother will make chicken soup.</u>

I imagine a big hen, flapping its wings.

Egypt
I wrap my tooth in some cotton or a tissue and take it outside. I say "Shining sun, shining sun, take this buffalo's tooth and bring me a bride's tooth." Then I throw the tooth high up, at the eye of the sun. (The Arabic word for bride is *aroussa*, which also means a candy or sweet.)

Libya

I throw my tooth at the sun and say, "Bring me a new tooth." My father tells me that I have a bright smile because my teeth come from the sun.

Morocco

I put my tooth under my pillow when I go to bed. The next morning I must rise with the sun and throw my tooth toward the sun while I say, "I give you a donkey's tooth and ask you to replace it with a gazelle's tooth." Otherwise, I might get donkey teeth.

Germany

I don't do anything special with my tooth.

Sweden

I put my tooth in a glass of water. In the morning my tooth will be gone and a coin will be in the glass.

Spain

I tuck my tooth under my pillow. While I am asleep, the little mouse called Ratoncito Perez will take my tooth and leave me money or candy in return.

Afghanistan

I drop my tooth inside a mouse hole, saying, "Take my dirty old tooth and give me your small clean one instead." ❖

Spain

Cameroon

Which tradition creates the strongest picture in your mind? Draw what you see. Then write a detailed caption.

✳ **Write about what you do when you lose a tooth.**

....

....

....

....

....

....

....

✳ **With a partner, discuss and create a new tradition for what to do with a lost tooth. Write about it below.**

....

....

....

....

....

....

....

....

✳ **Why do you think creating images in your mind is an important part of reading?**

Use details from
the text to create images
in your mind.

Yₒou can learn a lot about characters from the words they speak. When two characters talk together, it's called a **dialogue**.

In this fiction selection, Lucy Rose has a dialogue with Mr. Welsh, one of her teachers. Study the words carefully to help you imagine what Lucy Rose and Mr. Welsh are like and what they are feeling during the dialogue. As you read, underline words or phrases that create strong images for you. In the **Response Notes**, write about the images.

from Lucy Rose: Here's the Thing About Me by Katy Kelly

September 16

Here is one good thing: Today I got a postcard from my dad and on the front is a picture of a kid fishing and it says, "I thought I'd drop you a line!" On the back it says Miss Lucy Rose Reilly, which sounds older than 8, I think. Also there is a note that says: "Dear Lucy Rose, I hope your new school is swell. Is it? I love you, Dad."

My dad is a teacher of history at Ann Arbor Junior High School so he is one who wants to know every last thing about my school.

I made a postcard back. My grandmother gave it to me. It is not so interesting on the front because it just has a picture of the Lincoln Memorial which you can see anytime you want if you look at a penny. On the other side of the card, I wrote my old address and my dad's name and I called him Mr. Bob Reilly. Next to that I wrote: "Dear Dad, It's okay, I guess."

That was not the whole, exact truth.

Response Notes

September 22

One hard part about being an original thinker is that sometimes it makes teachers glare at you and Mrs. Washburn is a big one for glaring. Also she likes people to "STAY SEATED" just about all the time. When I explained about her at dinner last night, my grandfather said, "Mrs. Washburn doesn't have an original bone in her whole body."

Then my mom said, "It's only September and she might get better in a month or two." Which I doubt.

Luckily Mrs. Washburn is only a two-morning-a-week teacher who comes to help with reading.

My everyday teacher is Mr. Welsh and he does not glare. Today he came up to me at lunch and he said, "How are you settling in, Lucy Rose?"

And I said, "Okie-dokie."

And he said, "That's great."

And I said, "Well, a little okie-dokie."

"Only a little?" he asked me.

I told him, "Actually, it is not the easiest to be

the new kid in the neighborhood and the new kid at school at the exact same time especially when you don't know any friends yet."

He had sympathy for that because he told me, "I had a hard time when I was a new teacher and I didn't know any of the other teachers or any of the kids and, to tell you the truth, the principal made me a little nervous, but after a while it got better."

"Are you still nervous of the principal?"

"Nope," he said. "But it took a little time for me to get the hang of everything. I think that will be true for you, too."

"Doubt it," I said.

"Lucy Rose," Mr. Welsh said, "I'll eat my hat if things don't get better for you next month."

I have never seen him wear a hat so he might be kidding but I hope he is not because it is almost October and that is the next month and I would really like it to be better. ✦

* What are Lucy Rose and Mr. Welsh like? What images do you have of them? List the details from the selection that support your thoughts.

What is Lucy Rose like?	Details from the selection that support my thoughts

What is Mr. Welsh like?	Details from the selection that support my thoughts

✳ What is the most important information Mr. Welsh tells Lucy Rose? Explain.

....

....

....

....

....

....

....

✳ Why does Lucy Rose feel different from the other kids in her new school? Explain.

....

....

....

....

....

....

....

In a month's time, how might school have changed for Lucy Rose? Write a diary entry as Lucy Rose, telling how things have changed.

Studying a character's words helps you imagine what the character is like.

Authors sometimes use words that help readers use their **five senses**. These senses then trigger images. For example, what image do these words create? The water was icy cold. Maybe you thought of a swimming pool or just a cold glass of water. Words trigger different images for different people.

As you read the poem, underline words or phrases that help you use your senses. In the **Response Notes**, write about the senses you use and the images they create.

from Songs for the Seasons
by Jamake Highwater

Response Notes

The Sun sings gold in the pale sky of morning,
echoing across the summer hills.
His voice grows stronger as he rises,
spilling cascades of fire along the edges of the world.

Summer's song.
Hear the summer's sunshine song.

Now the summer days begin to fade.
The long and lingering evenings of August
diminish hour by hour.
The great Sun deserts the sky,
leaving an early darkness
where there had been a long, lean light.
Trees tremble in a northern breeze,
wrapped in leaves so hungry for the Sun
they carry tracings of his red and yellow light.

Autumn's song.
Hear the autumn's melancholy song. ❖

✳ **What words helped you "hear" the summer song?**

....

....

....

....

....

....

....

....

✳ **What words helped you "see" the season change from summer to fall?**

....

....

....

....

....

✳ **Why do you think summer has a sunshine song, and autumn has a melancholy song? Explain.**

....

....

....

....

....

....

....

✳ You read four selections in this unit. Talk to a partner about the images each selection created for you. Then write about the images.

Selection title	Images you remember
Hottest, Coldest, Highest, Deepest	
Throw Your Tooth on the Roof	
Lucy Rose: Here's the Thing About Me	
Songs for the Seasons	

When you read, use your senses to help create strong images and feelings.

Making Inferences

Your older brother is mixing flour, milk, and an egg in a big bowl. You see maple syrup on the table. "Yay!" you shout. "Pancakes for breakfast!"

You have just **made an inference**. You combined clues that you noticed with what you already know. The clues were the maple syrup and what your brother was mixing. You already know that pancakes are made with flour, milk, and eggs. You also know that your family likes maple syrup with pancakes.

You can make inferences when you read, too. An inference can be a prediction or a conclusion.

In this unit, you will read about different kinds of **relationships**. You will practice making inferences to better understand your reading.

Are you curious? Do you like to ask questions? If so, maybe you would like to become a scientist. Scientists ask questions and observe how the things around us behave.

As you read this nonfiction passage about scientists, underline phrases and sentences that show how scientists think and learn. In the **Response Notes**, write **inferences** about the ways they think and learn. An inference is a prediction or a conclusion.

Response Notes

They watch birds in the wild.

Scientists probably don't give up easily.

from How to Think Like a Scientist by Stephen Kramer

Scientists are people who are curious. They want to know about the things around them. They are always asking questions and trying to answer them.

Some scientists study birds. They might ask the question, "Why do meadowlarks sing?" Other scientists study objects in the universe. They might ask, "What happens to stars as they grow older?" Other scientists might ask: "What are atoms made of?" "How does gravity work?" "What lives at the bottom of the ocean?" "Why does the wind blow?" "How does the body heal itself?" Still other scientists might be interested in learning about old folktales and checking to see if any of them are true. Such a scientist might be interested in the question, "Can throwing a dead snake over a tree branch bring rain?"

Scientists believe that the things around us behave in certain ways. They believe that things that happen can be described by certain rules. Scientists try to find patterns in things. They look for explanations for the patterns in the things around us.

Scientists learn about things by observing and measuring them. Scientists can deal only with things that can be observed. To a scientist, being able to observe something means that we can learn about it by using our senses. It can be seen, heard, smelled, touched, or tasted.

Scientists often use instruments to help them make observations. Machines and special instruments can tell us much about things we can't know by using our senses alone. But if there is no way to observe and measure something, it can't be studied scientifically. ❖

✳ List three things you learned about how scientists think.

1. ....

2. ....

3. ....

✳ What can you infer, or conclude, about scientists from the way they think? Write your answer and then discuss it with a partner.

....

....

....

....

....

....

✳ Scientists learn about things in many different ways. Give an example of what a scientist might study when using these ways.

Scientific way of learning	What a scientist might study
Measuring	How far a bird can fly
Looking for patterns	
Using a microscope or other special instrument	
Using a machine	

✳ If scientists must observe things to learn about them, how do you think scientists know about dinosaur behavior? Dinosaurs have been extinct for thousands of years. Explain your thinking.

Use your questions and observations to make inferences.

Eugenie Clark is a world-famous **ichthyologist** (ik thee AHL uh jist). She is a scientist who studies sharks.

As you read this passage from Eugenie's **biography**, underline words and phrases that tell about the relationship between Eugenie and sharks. In the **Response Notes**, write **inferences** you make about the relationship. An inference is a prediction or a conclusion. Making inferences will help you better understand your reading.

Response Notes

She loved learning about sharks.

from Shark Lady: True Adventures of Eugenie Clark by Ann McGovern

Eugenie kept on learning new things from the sharks they caught on the shark lines. They caught hammer-heads, black-fin sharks, small dogfish sharks, lemon sharks, nurse sharks, bull sharks, and tiger sharks. Once in a while they caught a great white shark.

Eugenie's success in keeping sharks in captivity became known far and wide. Scientists from all over the world were coming to the lab to study sharks.

They cut open the stomachs of sharks to find out what sharks ate. They learned that sharks ate over 40 kinds of fish, including eels, stingrays, and other sharks. They found that sharks also ate octopus, crab, and shrimp. Sometimes they ate a sea turtle or a seabird or, once in a great while, a porpoise.

Eugenie found the most interesting part of her work was studying live sharks. She got to know the sharks so well that she could tell one shark from another by its behavior.

Eugenie wanted to learn more about their feeding habits. "How much food does it take to keep a nine-foot lemon shark alive?" Eugenie wondered. She learned that it took only two pounds of food a day to keep it healthy and active.

One day a Dr. Lester Aronson came to the lab. His work was the study of animal behavior.

"Has anyone ever made a study of the learning behavior of sharks?" Eugenie asked him.

He told her no. He said that everyone thought sharks were rather stupid.

"But you certainly have a good set-up here for testing to see if they could learn a simple task," he told her.

That was all she needed to hear. Before the day was over, they had worked out a plan.

First they designed the equipment to train the sharks. They made a wooden square and painted it white.

She will do an experiment to see if sharks are smart.

Eugenie placed the wooden square, called the target, into the shark pen. A shark had to learn that if it pressed its nose against the target, it would get food as a reward.

In a couple of months Eugenie's sharks learned to press the target every time they wanted food.

Then she made the test harder. First a shark had to press the target as usual. Then it had to turn and swim to the other end of the shark pen to get its reward.

Eugenie's plan worked! She proved that sharks could indeed learn a simple task.

One day toward the end of December, Eugenie learned something else about sharks. She set up her experiment as usual. But the sharks didn't press the target. Had they forgotten everything she had taught them? It turned out that sharks lost interest in food when the water got colder.

In February, when the water in the shark pen warmed up again, the sharks began once more to press the target for food, as if they had never lost a day of practice.

Now Eugenie knew that sharks were indeed smart enough to learn. And that they had a good memory as well! ❖

✳ **What is one inference you can make about Eugenie?
What clues in the text support it?**

Inference	Clues in the text

✳ **What is one inference you can make about sharks?
What clues in the text support it?**

Inference	Clues in the text

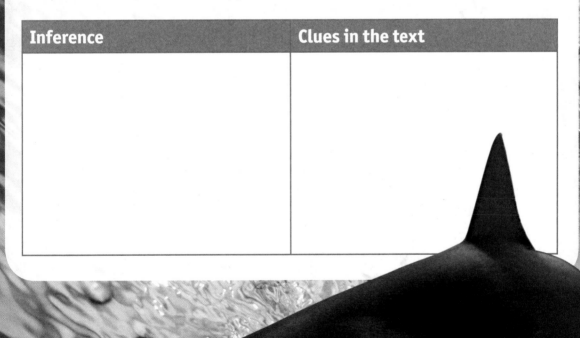

✳ List two important ideas you learned about Eugenie OR sharks. Tell why you think the ideas are important.

Important idea about Eugenie OR sharks	Why is it important?

✳ **Explain to a partner why making predictions and conclusions helps you better understand your reading. Write a few sentences about what you and your partner discussed.**

_____

_____

_____

_____

_____

_____

_____

Making inferences about a real scientist helps you better understand the scientist and the topic that he or she studies.

You can learn a lot about characters from the words they speak. When two characters talk together, it's called a **dialogue.**

In this fiction selection, Tomasito's father brings home a special bird. Tomasito isn't sure he likes the bird. As you read the dialogue between Tomasito and his father, underline words or phrases that help you **infer**, or figure out, what the characters are like. In the **Response Notes**, write your thoughts about the characters.

Response Notes

from Featherless Desplumado
by Juan Felipe Herrera

"A little pet, Tomasito. For you! Listen!" Papi sings as he shuts our trailer door. He stands next to me and peers into the cage he is carrying.

"Do you see him? The little bird with a bell hanging from his neck?" he says, pressing his bushy eyebrows against the crooked wire door.

"You mean the one with that grey pebble for a foot and tiny curled up leg? Is that . . . him?" I ask.

"He was born a little different, like you were," Papi whispers and pours some water for the little bird.

"Not like me—he doesn't have spina bifida! And he's featherless!" I say.

"Well, except for the fuzzy ring around his neck," Papi says, filling an old thimble with golden seeds. "You can call him *Desplumado.*"

"But Papi," I say, "If he doesn't have feathers, he can't fly!"

Tomasito doesn't understand why his father gave him a bird without feathers.

"Smile, Tomasito! Why so sad?" Marlena asks while we draw in class. She draws soccer balls with wings. I paint a volcano blowing up.

I lay my head on my desk. "Smiling is tough," I whisper. "As tough as making new friends. We just moved here. Back in Mendota, I knew everyone. Now, everybody asks me all over again why I'm in a wheelchair."

"Why, Tomasito? Why, why, why?" she asks, to make me laugh a little.

"See, I told you!" I say, "When I was born, my spinal cord wasn't completely formed."

Marlena gives me her drawing. "Friends?" she asks.

Tonight Papi comes home from work at the Pinedale Motel. He tiptoes to my bed and kisses me good night.

I look up at a tiny star outside my window. I wish I could fly into the star's circle of light. I wish I could swing on one of its electric wings.

Cooo. Cooo, coooooo. The featherless bird cries long cooing sounds from the far corner of my room. Cooo, cooo . . .

I plug my ears and don't listen. ✦

✳ **What can you infer about Tomasito and his father from their dialogue? Write your thoughts in the chart.**

My inferences about Tomasito:

My inferences about Papi:

✳ **Why do you think Tomasito wishes he could "fly into the star's circle of light"?**

....

....

....

....

....

....

....

✳ **Why do you think Tomasito plugs his ears and tries not to listen to the cooing of the bird?**

....

....

....

....

....

....

....

* Think about Tomasito's feelings at this point in the story. Write a letter that he might write to a friend back in Mendota.

Dear _____ ,

_____

_____

Yours,

Tomasito

Making inferences from dialogue helps you understand what the characters are like.

In a story, a character often changes from the beginning to the end. Thinking about what a character says and does will help you better understand the changes that happen.

As you read more about Tomasito, underline words and phrases that show you he's changing.

In the **Response Notes**, write **inferences** about the changes you see. An inference is a prediction or a conclusion.

from Featherless Desplumado
by Juan Felipe Herrera

Under the morning sun, Papi waits with me for my school bus.

"You've been grumpy all morning," he says, "You didn't want to eat, didn't want to go to school. What is it, Tomasito?"

"At school nobody ever invites me to play! At recess, I sit alone and count soccer balls slamming into the net!"

"Things take time, Tomasito. *Paciencia*," Papi says. The chairlift screeches and jerks me into the bus. Patience?

On the soccer field, Coach Gordolobo blows the whistle. "We are the Fresno Flyers!" shouts Marlena as she throws her arm around the goalie.

"Not me, I'm from Mendota, remember?" I yell from the sidelines. I look down at my wheelchair. Flyers?

After the game, I push-push and huff over to Marlena. "You want to play?" she asks. "But I can't kick the ball," I say. "Be a Flyer!" she says. "Use your wings!"

Wings? Does she mean my wheelchair?

At night, in our trailer, I pull a feather from my pillow and place it at the pebble foot of the featherless bird.

Response Notes

He's starting to think that maybe he CAN play.

He's really
trying now.

"This is so your toes will warm up, and maybe your own feathers will grow," I say as I stroke Desplumado's scrunchy leg.

Windy clouds swirl around the moon like a soccer net of mist.

"Fresno Flyers! Practice! Let's go!" Marlena yells from the soccer field.

Kids race across the grass, swooping like kites above an emerald sea.

<u>No one notices how fast I spin my wheels. Will I ever catch up? Will they ever see me?</u>

After practice, Coach Gordolobo says, "Junior Resortes, our fastest runner, has the flu. What should we do?"

"What about Tomasito?" Marlena winks at me.

"Tomasito who?" Coach asks.

"Me!" I say. "From Mendota!"

"You?" Coach wrinkles his forehead.

"You?" everyone echoes.

I spin the ball fast on my head. Coach thinks hard and fast for a minute.

Then, "You're in, Tomasito." He pats me on the back.

In the game. The ball is up. My head stretches out-out, like Desplumado's prickly head.

Zaz! I didn't know my head could do that! But I miss the goal.

"Good *cabeza* shot, Tomasito!" Marlena shouts.

I didn't know I could play soccer! My hands are red and sore from zigzagging my wheely across the hot field. Zwoop! Marlena slams the ball to me—Zaz! I almost make a wobbly *cabeza*-goal.

"*Ajúa!*" I shout out loud. ✤

❋ **Look at the chart below. For each character's words or actions, write what you infer or learn about them.**

Character's words or actions	What you infer or learn about the character
Papi: "Things take time."	Papi is patient.
Marlena: "Use your wings!"	
Tomasita: "This is so your toes will warm up, and maybe your own feathers will grow."	
Coach: He wrinkles his forehead.	

✳ How did Tomasito change from the beginning to the end of the story? How did your inferences help you better understand his changes?

....

....

....

....

....

....

....

....

✳ Why did Tomasito change?

....

....

....

....

....

....

....

....

✳ **What was your favorite part of the story? Draw a picture of it and write a caption below.**

✴ In this unit, you read—

- *How to Think Like a Scientist*
- *Shark Lady: True Adventures of Eugenie Clark*
- *Featherless Desplumado*

With which selection was it easiest to make inferences? Discuss your thoughts with a partner. Then write how making inferences helped you better understand this selection.

Think about what a character says and does. This will help you understand how and why a character changes in a story.

Synthesizing

Have you ever been surprised by a book or story? Maybe you thought it would be scary, but it turned out to be funny.

Readers often change their thoughts about a story between the beginning and the end. Readers also create new thoughts about a story after they've read it. When readers notice how their thoughts change and grow, they are **synthesizing** their thoughts.

In this unit, you will read about different kinds of **journeys.** You will practice synthesizing your thoughts to better understand your reading.

113

What makes a story fun to read? Maybe the **characters** are interesting, the **conflict** is exciting, or the **setting** is unusual. Every story is different, and every reader likes something different. But every story has the same **elements**.

- characters: the people or animals in a story

- setting: where and when the story takes place

- plot: a series of events

- conflict: the problem in the story

- resolution: how the problem gets solved

When you know the elements of a story, you will better understand the story and be able to write a meaningful summary of it.

As you read this passage from *Flat Stanley*, look for and underline details that help you identify the characters, setting, plot, conflict, and resolution. In the **Response Notes**, write what the details tell you.

I see three names.
I think the story has
three characters.

from Flat Stanley by Jeff Brown

One day Stanley got a letter from his friend Thomas Anthony Jeffrey, whose family had moved recently to California. A school vacation was about to begin, and Stanley was invited to spend it with the Jeffreys.

"Oh, boy!" Stanley said. "I would love to go!"

Mr. Lambchop sighed. "A round-trip train or airplane ticket to California is very expensive," he said. "I will have to think of some cheaper way."

When Mr. Lambchop came home from the office that evening, he brought with him an enormous brown-paper envelope.

"Now then, Stanley," he said. "Try this for size."

The envelope fit Stanley very well. There was even room left over, Mrs. Lambchop discovered, for an egg-salad sandwich made with thin bread, and a toothbrush case filled with milk.

They had to put a great many stamps on the envelope to pay for both airmail and insurance, but it was still much less expensive than a train or airplane ticket to California.

The next day Mr. and Mrs. Lambchop slid Stanley into his envelope, along with the egg-salad sandwich and the toothbrush case full of milk, and mailed him from the box on the corner. The envelope had to be folded to fit through the slot, but Stanley was a limber boy, and inside the box he straightened right up again.

Mrs. Lambchop was nervous because Stanley had never been away from home alone before. She rapped on the box.

"Can you hear me, dear?" she called. "Are you all right?"

Stanley's voice came quite clearly. "I'm fine. Can I eat my sandwich now?"

"Wait an hour. And try not to get overheated, dear," Mrs. Lambchop said. Then she and Mr. Lambchop cried out, "Good-bye, good-bye!" and went home.

Stanley had a fine time in California. When the visit was over, the Jeffrey's returned him in a beautiful white envelope they had made themselves. It had red-and-blue markings to show that it was airmail, and Thomas Jeffrey had lettered it "Valuable" and "Fragile" and "This End Up" on both sides.

Back home Stanley told his family that he had been handled so carefully he never felt a single bump. Mr. Lambchop said it proved that jet planes were wonderful, and so was the Postal Service, and that this was a great age in which to live.

Stanley thought so too. ❖

The problem is that Stanley wants to go to California, but a train or plane ticket is too expensive.

THIS END UP

FRAGILE

TO: _____

VALUABLE

❋ What are the story elements in *Flat Stanley*? Look over the selection and your Response Notes to help you fill in the chart.

Who are the characters?	
What is the setting? (There may be more than one.)	
What is the conflict or problem?	
What are some of the events, in the order they happened?	
How is the problem resolved?	

❋ Write a radio advertisement for *Flat Stanley* that includes the most important details about all the story elements. Read your ad to the class.

✳ **Where would you mail yourself if you could? Explain why you chose this place.**

....

....

....

....

....

....

....

....

....

When you summarize a story, include important details about the characters, setting, plot, conflict, and resolution.

AIR MAIL

Every character has a **point of view**, or a way of looking at things. When you study a character's point of view, you can learn a lot about him or her.

In *Selene Goes Home*, the main character is a cat. How do you think a cat sees the world? As you read, underline words and phrases that show you Selene's point of view. In the **Response Notes**, write what you learn about Selene.

from Selene Goes Home by Lucy Diggs

Response Notes

Selene sat up on the hill and watched the house. For hours and hours the men went back and forth, carrying boxes and furniture out of the house and packing them into a truck. Selene was worried. Nothing like this had ever happened before. What was going to happen next?

In the afternoon the men closed up the back of the truck and drove away. When the truck disappeared down the driveway, Selene decided it was safe to go back inside the house. But nothing inside the house was the way it was supposed to be. In the living room, only the rug remained. In the dining room, only the big sideboard. In the bedroom, nothing except a large spiderweb in the corner of the closet. Selene was too upset to enjoy this discovery. She went to the kitchen. Nothing in the kitchen. Even her bowl was gone. Now what would she do for dinner? Meowing mournfully, Selene went into the living room to curl up in her bed in the window seat. All the soft, cozy pillows were gone. She jumped into the window seat and settled uncomfortably on the hard boards.

"Selene!" Margaret called. "Here, kitty, kitty!"

Selene almost jumped down to cuddle in Margaret's arms, but then she decided it would be more prudent to wait and see what was on Margaret's mind. Her voice had a shrill note to it, and that usually meant she was going to do something that Selene didn't enjoy—like sprinkle her with flea powder or trim her claws or give her a bath.

Oh no! Margaret was holding the cat carrier. Selene hissed at it. That carrier meant trouble. Margaret would stuff her inside and take her to the vet. In the vet's waiting room, it stank of dog and stranger-cats, of medicine and antiseptic. In the examining room it was even worse. The vet poked her with his hands and jabbed her with needles.

Hissing at the carrier turned out to be a mistake, because it made Margaret look in her direction.

"There you are, Selene. Come, kitty, kitty, kitty!"

Selene jumped down and ran for it, but Margaret caught her and stuck her in the carrier. She took her out to the car and put her in the backseat.

Selene yowled in misery. She yowled while Margaret backed the car around and drove down the driveway. She yowled when the car turned onto the street. She yowled while the car rolled along the road. At last the car came to a stop and she yowled even louder, thinking about the dogs and the horrible smells at the vet's.

Margaret lifted the carrier out of the car and Selene forgot to yowl. What a strange smell! It wasn't the vet's. What was it? ❖

How is Selene's point of view about moving different from Margaret's? Write your thoughts in the chart.

Selene's point of view	Margaret's point of view
She didn't know why the men were carrying boxes. She was scared and confused.	She knew exactly why the men were carrying boxes. She was moving!

✳ What are some of the most important ideas
the author wants you to understand about
Selene? What does the author want you to
think at the end of the story? These big ideas
are your synthesis.

....

....

....

....

....

....

✳ What bigger message about life, in general,
might the author be trying to give you? Explain.

....

....

....

....

....

....

※ **How did your thoughts about Selene or Stanley change as you read each story from beginning to end?**

....

....

....

....

....

....

....

....

....

....

....

....

....

....

Thinking about a character's point of view will help you discover big ideas about the character.

What are some of your strongest memories from when you were little? What do these memories tell you about yourself? Studying a character's memories in a selection can lead you to big ideas about the character and the selection.

In this two-part poem, the **narrator** recalls his family trips to visit his grandmother in Mexico. As you read, underline words and phrases that tell about the narrator's memories. In the **Response Notes**, write questions or comments about the memories.

Response Notes

1. From the Bellybutton of the Moon

by Francisco X. Alarcón

> whenever
> I say
> "Mexico"
>
> I feel
> the same wind
> on my face
>
> I felt when
> I would open
> the window
>
> on my first
> trip south
> by car
>
> I see
> Atoyac
> again
>
> the town
> where my mother
> was raised

and I spent
summer
vacations

I hear
familiar
voices

laughter
greetings
farewells

I smell
my grandma's
gardenias

2. From the Bellybutton of the Moon

whenever
I say
"Mexico"

I hear
my grandma
telling me

about the Aztecs
and the city
they built

on an island
in the middle
of a lake

"Mexico"
says
my grandma

"means: from
the bellybutton
of the moon"

"don't forget
your origin
my son"

maybe
that's
why

whenever
I now say
"Mexico"

I feel
like touching
my bellybutton ✤

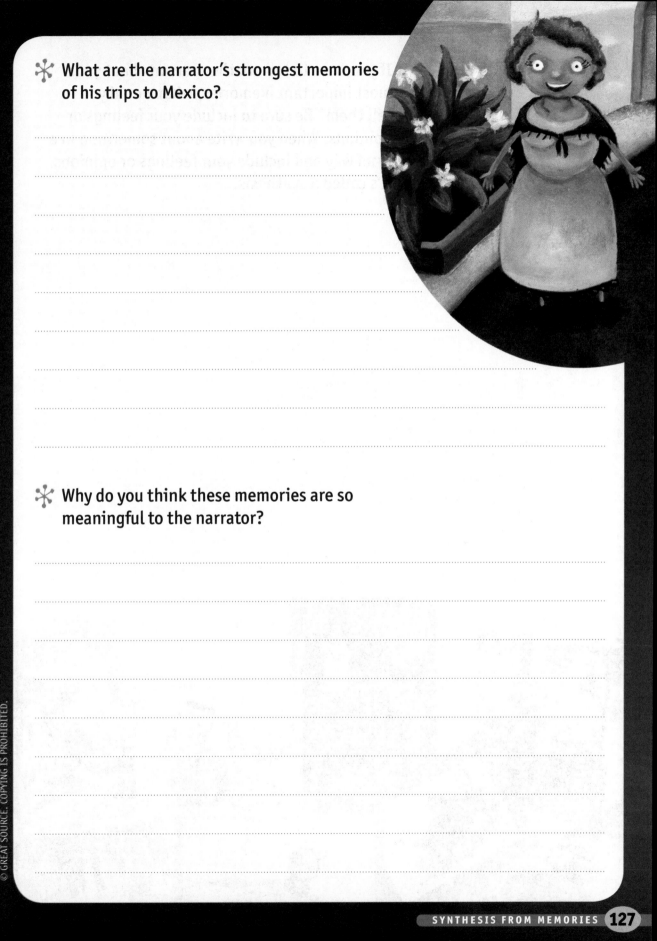

✳ **What are the narrator's strongest memories of his trips to Mexico?**

....
....
....
....
....
....

✳ **Why do you think these memories are so meaningful to the narrator?**

....
....
....
....
....
....
....

✳ If you were to tell another person about your most important memories, what would you tell them? Be sure to include your feelings or opinions. When you write about something in a brief way and include your feelings or opinions, it's called a synthesis.

✳ **Plan and write a diary entry about a memorable trip or vacation you've taken. Include why it is so memorable.**

Thinking about a character's memories can lead you to big ideas about the character and the selection.

Authors and poets often use **sensory details** in their writing. Sensory details are details that spark a reader's sense of sight, sound, taste, smell, or touch.

In this poem about a polar bear's journey, look for and underline details that spark your senses. Thinking about sensory details in the poem will lead you to **synthesize** big ideas about the poem.

In the **Response Notes**, draw or write what the sensory details help you see in your mind.

from Great Crystal Bear by Carolyn Lesser

Great crystal bear,
How do you survive on the thick ice
Covering the deep Arctic sea?
As you pad through the storm wind,
Veils of snow race past your fringy paws.
Time to scoop a hollow in a drift
And huddle in,
Back to the wind,
Nose pushed under the snow,
Paws snuggling your body.
Winds howl. Snow swirls,
Covering you like dust until you vanish.
Sleep warm, crystal bear.

The earth leans far from the sun
As you rouse from your drift-bed
This winter solstice morning.
How lucky that every other day of the year
Each hollow hair of your fur
Gathers sunlight
To hear your black skin and thick layer of fat.
Your blubbery blanket keeps you warm
For long, dog-paddling swims
And months of day-and-night
Winter wandering.

As you wander, great bear,
Your keen nose smells
Bear friends and relatives nearby.
Some nap behind hills of ice.
Others travel.
They are like you,
Comforted by the scent of companions
But on singular journeys,
Alone, but not lonely.

✳ **Write two phrases from the poem that you visualize well. Describe what each one makes you see in your mind.**

Phrase you visualize well	What the phrase makes you see in your mind
Veils of snow race past your fringy paws	I see sheets of snow blowing by a bear with really long claws.

✳ List three facts you learned about polar bears from the poem.

1. ....

....

2. ....

....

3. ....

....

✳ Think about the sensory details in the poem, and the facts you learned about polar bears. What big ideas can you create that describe a polar bear's life? These ideas are your synthesis.

....

....

....

....

....

....

❋ **How does thinking about big ideas, and your feelings or opinions about them, help you better understand a selection?**

✳ In this unit, you read about four different journeys. What are the journeys? List one big idea about each one.

■ What is the journey in *Flat Stanley*?

....

....

....

■ What is one big idea from the selection?

....

....

....

■ What is the journey in *Selene Goes Home*?

....

....

....

■ What is one big idea from the selection?

....

....

■ What is the journey in "From the Bellybutton of the Moon"?

....

....

....

■ What is one big idea from the selection?

....

....

....

■ What is the journey in "Great Crystal Bear"?

....

....

....

■ What is one big idea from the selection?

....

....

Thinking about
the sensory details in a poem
will lead you to big ideas
about the poem.

A

advertisement a notice published in a newspaper or magazine

amateur not professional; for people who are not very experienced

Antarctica the continent that includes the South Pole

atoms the smallest bits of matter

B

barbershop place where men get their hair cut

behavior how a person or an animal acts

boisterous noisy, lively

C

captivity being kept in an environment other than nature

cascades waterfalls

chairlift a motorized platform on a car, van, or bus that raises and lowers a wheelchair

Chiang Jiang a major river in China

Chinatown an area in a city where people from China live

classical music that was written long ago

D

dribble bouncing a basketball rapidly and repeatedly

drop you a line an expression that means "write to you"

E

energetic full of energy; lively

engulfed covered, took over

equipment tools, supplies

eventually at a later time

F

familiar something you know

farewells goodbyes

feasted on enjoyed very much

ferocious violent or dangerous

flickering with lights or flames going on and off

fossils impressions of plants or animals that are preserved in rocks

fragile easily broken

gardenias flowers with a perfumed smell
gazelle a small deer-like animal found in Africa and Asia
glare to look at sternly
glide move smoothly
gravity the force that pulls things to the center of the Earth
greetings ways of saying hello

hesitate wait
Hong Kong a region of the People's Republic of China
hookballs shooting a basketball into the basket in a curving motion

ignore pay no attention to
I'll eat my hat an expression that means "I don't believe it's possible"
instrument a tool that makes music
insurance something you pay in case a letter is lost or damaged

jumpshot jumping off the floor and shooting a ball into the basket at the same time
knowledge what people know
lack not have
layups running toward the basket and putting the ball in at the last moment
lingering staying a long time
lounge a waiting area; a room where people socialize

melancholy sad
mournfully sadly
nervous not calm, unable to relax
newsprint type of paper on which newspapers are printed
numb not able to feel anything

O

obsidian a glass stone formed by the cooling of lava
okie-dokie a funny way to say "OK"
origin where you came from

P

pale light-colored

peers stares carefully

perseverance the act of sticking with
    something

pickled kumquats small citrus fruits
    preserved in vinegar

plug close up with your fingers

poisonous deadly

presses large machines used in printing
    newspapers and books

pressroom room where the presses are
    kept, room where reporters gather

prudent careful

Q R

quantities amounts

Ratoncito Spanish for "little mouse"

realize understand

roaring moving quickly and with a lot
    of energy

rouse get up

S

scarcely hardly; almost not

screeches makes a loud high-pitched
    sound

shafts columns

shuddered shook

singular done alone, without any help

slumped sat in a droopy way

span the distance between the ends
    of something

spewing spitting out

superintendent a boss, a person
    in charge

T

tacking putting up with pins or tacks

target a special spot, a mark for aiming at

timid shy, afraid

V W Y

valuable worth a lot

vanish disappear

veils coverings, like curtains

venom a poison that a snake, spider, or
    insect injects into its victim

Vostok a Russian research station near
    the South Pole

winked closed and opened one eye quickly

wobbly shaky

word got out people started talking

yowled meowed loudly

ACKNOWLEDGMENTS

8 "Chef Huey" from *The Stories Huey Tells* by Ann Cameron. Copyright © 1995. Reprinted with permission of Alfred A. Knopf.

16 From *The Boy on Fairfield Street* by Kathleen Krull. Copyright © 2004. Reprinted with permission by Random House Children's Books.

20 From *Once Upon a Time in Chicago* by Jonah Winter. Copyright © 2000. Reprinted with permission by Hyperion Books for Children.

25 From 26 *Fairmont Avenue* by Tomie dePaola, copyright © 1999 by Tomie dePaola. Used by permission of G.P. Putnam's Sons, A Division of Penguin Young Readers Group, A Member of Penguin Group (USA) Inc., 345 Hudson Street, New York, NY 10014. All rights reserved.

29 "Basketball Star", from *My Daddy is a Cool Dude And Other Poems* by Karama Fufuka, copyright © 1975 by Karama Fufuka. Used by permission of Dial Books for Young Readers, A Division of Penguin Young Readers Group, A Member of Penguin Group (USA) Inc., 345 Husdon Street, New York, NY 10014. All rights reserved.

30 "Growing Up" from *The Little Hill* by Harry Behn. Copyright © 1949 by Harry Behn, renewed 1977 by Alice L. Behn.

34 From *Donovan's Word Jar* by Monalisa DeGross. Copyright © 1994. Reprinted with permission by HarperCollins Publishers.

39 "Tradition" from *Under the Sunday Tree* by Eloise Greenfield. Copyright ©1988. Reprinted with permission by HarperTrophy, a division of HarperCollins Publishers.

43, 47 © 2003 by Myron Uhlberg from *The Printer*, written by Myron Uhlberg, illustrated by Henri Sorenson, and published by Peachtree Publishers. Permission to reprint granted by Peachtree Publishers.

54 From *Rock Secrets* by Betsy James. Reprinted by permission of Cricket Magazine Group, Carus Publishing Company, from CLICK magazine May/June 2005, Vol. 8, No. 5, text and art © 2005 by Betsy James

57 From *Real Live Monsters!* by Ellen Schecter. Copyright ©1995. Reprinted with permission by Bantam Books.

60 "In Hong Kong" from *My Chinatown* by Kam Mak. Copyright ©2002. Reprinted with permission by HarperCollins Publishers.

64 From *Sarah, Plain and Tall* by Patricia MacLachlan. Copyright © 1985. Reprinted with permission by HarperTrophy, a division of HarperCollins Publishers.

70 Excerpt from *Hottest, Coldest, Highest, Deepest* by Steve Jenkins. Copyright © 1998 by Steve Jenkins. Reprinted by permission of Houghton Mifflin Company. All rights reserved.

76 Excerpts from *Throw Your Tooth on the Roof: Tooth Traditions from Around the World* by Selby B. Beeler, illustrated by G. Brian Karas. Text copyright © 1998 by Selby B. Beeler. Illustrations copyright © 1998 by G. Brian Karas. Reprinted by permission of Houghton Mifflin Company. All rights reserved.

81 From *Lucy Rose Here's The Thing About Me* by Katy Kelly. Illustrated by Adam Rex, copyright © 2004 by Katy Kelly. Used by permission of Random House Children's Books, a division of Random House, Inc.

87 From *Songs for the Seasons* by Jamake Highwater. Copyright © 1995. Reprinted with permission by Lothrop, Lee, & Shepard Books.

92 From *How to Think Like a Scientist* by Stephen Kramer. Copyright ©1987. Reprinted with permission by Thomas Y. Crowell.

96 From *Shark Lady: True Adventures of Eugenie Clark* by Ann McGovern. Copyright © 1978 by Ann McGovern. Reprinted by permission of Scholastic, Inc.

102, 107 Reprinted with permission of the publisher, Children's Book Press, San Francisco, CA, www.childrensbookpress.org. From *Featherless/Desplumado*. Story copyright © 2004 by Children's Book Press.

114 From *Flat Stanley* by Jeff Brown. Copyright © 1964, renewed 1992 by Jeff Brown. Reprinted with permission by Scholastic, Inc.

119 Reprinted with the permission of Atheneum Books for Young Readers, an imprint of Simon & Schuster Children's Publishing Division from *Selene Goes Home* by Lucy Diggs. Text copyright © 1989 Lucy Diggs.

124 Reprinted with permission of the publisher, Children's Book Press, San Francisco, CA, www.childrensbookpress.org. From *The Bellybutton of the Moon and other Summer Poems*. Poem copyright © 1998 Children's Book Press.

130 From *Great Crystal Bear*, text copyright © 1996 by Carolyn Lesser, reprinted with permission from Harcourt, Inc.

CREDITS

ILLUSTRATIONS

3–7: Pablo Bernasconi; **8–13:** Sophie Lewandowski; **15:** Pablo Bernasconi; **16, 17:** Mary Anne Lloyd; **21:** Mike Litwin; **26:** Lee Calderon; **30:** Andrew Rowland; **32:** Lee Calderon; **33:** Pablo Bernasconi; **34, 36:** Ken Gamage; **43:** Mike Litwin; **53:** Pablo Bernasconi; **64–68:** Andrew Rowland; **69:** Pablo Bernasconi; **70–72:** Jean Wisenbaugh; **75:** © P_Wei/istockphoto; **77, 78:** Lee Calderon; **81–83:** Ken Gamage; **84:** © Rouska Dimitrova/istockphoto; **85:** Ken Gamage; **86:** © Rouska Dimitrova/istockphoto; **90:** Ken Gamage; **91:** Pablo Bernasconi; **95:** Justin Parpan; **102–107:** Annie Lunsford; **110 t:** Annie Lunsford; **113:** Pablo Bernasconi; **114, 115:** Andrew Rowland; **124–127:** Lee Calderon

PHOTOGRAPHY

Photo Research by AARTPACK, Inc.

Cover: © Gary S Chapman/The Image Bank/Getty Images; **1:** © Gary S Chapman/The Image Bank/Getty Images

Unit 1 116: © James L. Amos/CORBIS; **18t:** © Bananastock/Jupiter Images; **18b:** © saw/istockphoto; **20t:** © Bettmann/CORBIS; **20b:** © small tom/Fotolia; **22t:** © AVTG/istockphoto; **22b:** © Underwood & Underwood/CORBIS; **23:** © Ashley Whitworth/Fotolia; **24:** © AVTG/istockphoto; **25:** © Andersen Ross/Blend Images/Jupiter Images; **28:** © Inti St Clair/Digital Vision/Getty Images; **29t:** © Mira/Alamy; **29b:** © Polka Dot Images/Jupiter Images; **30:** © Jo Ann Snover/Fotolia; **31:** © Mathew Hayward/Fotolia

Unit 2 35b: © Douglas Stevens/Fotolia; **35 tacs:** © Luis Carlos Torres/istockphoto; **37:** © Jan Tyler/istockphoto; **37b:** © Bananastock/Jupiter Images; **38:** © Jan Tyler/istockphoto; **39t:** © Tom Nebbia/CORBIS; **39l:** © levgenia Tikhonova/istockphoto; **39r:** © John Carleton/Fotolia; **39b:** © Sergey Shlyaev/Fotolia; **40:** © Digital Vision/Getty Images; **41t:** © Tom Stewart/CORBIS; **41b:** © Farhad Parsa/zefa/Corbis; **44:** © Sam Aronov/istockphoto; **45t:** © Glen Jones/istockphoto; **45:** © dotshock/Fotolia; **46:** © dotshock/Fotolia; **47t:** © sylvaine thomas/Fotolia; **47b:** © Photodisc/InMagine; **48t:** © Stockdisc Classic/Alamy; **48b:** © Andreea Manciu/Istockphoto; **49:** © dotshock/Fotolia; **49r:** © Ludovic Moulin/Graphistock/Jupiter Images; **50b:** © Nicholas Prior/Taxi/Getty Images; **50t:** © Wolfgang Kraus/Fotolia; **51:** © Wolfgang Kraus/Fotolia; **51c:** © Stefan Klein/istockphoto; **52:** © Andreea Manciu/Istockphoto; **52l:** © Stockbyte/Getty Images; **52r:** © Richard Scherznger/istockphoto

Unit 3 54: © Ed Bock/CORBIS; **55r:** © Tara Flake/istockphoto; **55b:** © Mike Bentley/istockphoto; **56l:** © Siede Preis/Photodisc/Getty Images; **56:** © Mike Bentley/istockphoto; **57t:** © JOHN MITCHELL/OSF/Animals Animals - Earth Scenes **57c:** © Soubrette/istockphoto; **57b:** © Edyta Cholcha-Cisowska/istockphoto; **58t:** © Edyta Cholcha-Cisowska/istockphoto; **58br:** © Edyta Cholcha-Cisowska/istockphoto; **58b:** © blindelinse/istockphoto; **59:** © Jaroslav Machacek/Fotolia; **60t:** © Kaz Chiba/Photographer's Choice/Getty Images; **60b:** © PhotoLink/Photodisc/Getty Images; **61:** © ImageShop/Corbis; **62:** © ImageShop/Corbis; **63:** © Hill Street Studios/Blend Images/Getty Images; **65:** © Rodion Sharipov/

istockphoto; **66:** © tracy tucker/istockphoto;
68: © blindelinse/istockphoto; **68t:** © Tara Flake/
istockphoto; **68tc:** © Edyta Cholcha-Cisowska/
istockphoto; **68bc:** © ImageShop/Corbis

Unit 4   70: © Tomasz Walas/Fotolia;
72: © Michelle Eadie/istockphoto; **73t:** © Marina
Gribok/Fotolia; **73b:** © Maxime VIGE/istockphoto;
74: © pomortzeff/istockphoto; **76:** © Notebook/
Fotolia; **77:** © Jan Rysavy/istockphoto;
78: © Marina Gribok/Fotolia; **79:** © Philip Dyer/
istockphoto; **80:** © Nick Schlax/istockphoto;
86: © Feng Yu/Fotolia; **87:** © PNC/Digital
Vision/Getty Images; **87:** © ILLYCH/istockphoto;
88b: © dieter Spears/istockphoto; **88t:** © Betsy
Dupuis/istockphoto; **89:** © Andrea Gingerich/
istockphoto; **89t:** © ILLYCH/istockphoto;
89b: © Emilia Stasiak/istockphoto; **90b:** © Betsy
Dupuis/istockphoto; **90:** © Andrea Gingerich/
istockphoto

Unit 5   92: © Hinata Kusakabe/ailead/
amana images/Getty Images; **93:** © American
Images Inc./Digital Vision/Getty Images;
94t: © blaneyphoto/istockphoto;
94b: © Andreea Manciu/istockphoto;
95: © amast606/Fotolia; **96t:** © John
Pendygraft-St.Petersburg Times;
96b: © Tom Grill/Iconica/Getty Images;
97: © David Doubilet/National Geographic;
98: © David Doubilet; **99:** © Selahattin
BAYRAM/istockphoto; **99b:** © Jeff
Hunter/Photographer's Choice RF/Getty
Images; **101:** © Cliff Parnell/istockphoto;
104: © Royalty-Free/Corbis; **105:** © Christophe
Penninckx/Fotolia; **105t:** © Carl & Ann
Purcell/CORBIS; **106l:** © Igor Negovelov/
Fotolia; **106t:** © Marko Beric/Fotolia;

106b: © nicholas belton/istockphoto;
107b: © Sokol, Howard/Index Stock Imagery/
Jupiter Images; **108:** © nikada33/istockphoto;
109: © nikada33/istockphoto; **111:** © Didier
Kobi/Fotolia; **112:** © Comstock Images/Jupiter
Images

Unit 6   116: © Dena Steiner/istockphoto;
117: © Sean Justice/Corbis; **118t** © Lise
Gagne/istockphoto; **118b:** © Tetra Images/
Corbis; **118:** © Stephen Green/istockphoto;
119: © Nicolas Mercier/Fotolia; **120l:** © Lew
Robertson/Corbis; **120r:** © DLILLC/Corbis;
121: © Massimiliano Pieraccini/Fotolia;
122t: © Inmagine; **122:** © Korel Mor/
Fotolia; 122bl: © Tony Campbell/Fotolia;
122br: © Sergey Shlyaev/Fotolia; **123:** © Korel
Mor/Fotolia; **123t:** © Zoran Stojkovic/
Fotolia; **127:** © Krystian Polak; **Clockwise
in order from a to j. 128a:** © Ariel Skelley/
Blend Images/Jupiter Images; **128b:** © Nic
Taylor/istockphoto; **128c:** © digitalskillet/
istsockphoto; **128d:** © Lisa F. Young/
istockphoto; **128e:** © philippe Devanne/
Fotolia; **128f:** © Mikhail Tolstoy/Fotolia;
128g: © Joson/zefa/Corbis; **128h:** © Stéphane
Hette/Fotolia; **128i:** © Jose Manuel
Gelpi Diaz/Fotolia; **128j:** © Diana
Rich/Istockphoto;**129:** © Diana Rich/
Istockphoto; **130t:** © Wolfgang Kaehler/
CORBIS; **130b:** © Theo Allofs/zefa/Corbis;
131: © Kennan Ward/CORBIS; **132:** © Layne
Kennedy/Corbis; **132:** © Daniel J. Cox/CORBIS;
133: © Jeff Vanuga/CORBIS; **133t:** © Jenny
E. Ross/Corbis; **133b:** © Jenny E. Ross/Corbis;
134l: © Andres Rodriguez/Fotolia; **134:** © Korel
Mor/Fotolia; **135:** © Pinar Caglayan/Fotolia;
136: © Yanik Chauvin/Fotolia

INDEX